Mommy and Daddy have a lock on the cabinet. That way, we do not go and get snacks anytime we want, since snack time is our favorite time of the day.

IT'S SNACK TIME

Majida Conteh

Morenikeh Conteh

JOURNAL JOY

An Imprint of Journal Joy Publishers

www.thejournaljoy.com

Copyright © 2021 by Majida Conteh and Morenikeh Conteh

An *Imprint* of Journal Joy *Publishers*

All rights reserved. Printed in the United States of America. No part of this book may be reproduced, distributed, or transmitted in any form or by any means, without the prior written permission of the authors, except in the case of brief quotations embodied in critical reviews and certain other noncommercial uses permitted by copyright law.

For information on publishing, contact Journal Joy at Info@thejournaljoy.com.

www.thejournaljoy.com

Summary: Two sisters share their favorite time of day; Snack Time. It's Snack Time brings all readers back to the best part of the day, whether at school or home as a child. Grab your child with their favorite snack and enjoy!

ISBN: 978-1-7361688-1-3

Edited by: Riel Felice

Pictures by: Nimrah Saleem

Author Email: contehmmc@outlook.com

First paperback edition, 2021

DEDICATION

This book is dedicated to all of the children that have younger siblings and what happens when you leave your snack around. This book is teaching children that although you may have been upset over a situation it is important to not stay mad and enjoy your favorite meal together with each other.

My sister and I love when it is snack time. We have a special cabinet in the kitchen where our snacks are stored.

When we want snacks, we ask Mommy or Daddy to get them for us.

Today, I think I am going to get a Nutri-Grain bar. My sister decided to get a Nutri-Grain bar, too.

Looks like we are both going to eat the same snack!

After Mommy gave us our snacks, we went into the living room and watched television while we ate our snacks.

While I was eating my snack, I was watching television.

I took a bite of my snack and placed it on the couch. When I reached for my snack again, I realized that my sister had eaten it.

I called out for Mommy.

"Mommy! Mommy! Nikeh ate my snack."

When Mommy came into the living room, she asked Nikeh why she ate my snack. Nikeh just looked at Mommy with her mouth full.

I started to cry because I was very upset. I did not like that my sister ate my snack.

While I was crying, my sister walked away from me and continued to eat my snack. I then kindly asked Mommy if I could have another snack.

Mommy gave me another snack and told me not to leave it on the couch again.

After Mommy gave me my snack, I went to the living room again. This time, I held my snack while watching television.

While I was eating my snack, I decided to share it with my little sister. I gave her a piece of my snack. I told Mommy that I shared my snack with my sister.

"That was very nice of you, Majida," she said.

I love sharing my snacks with my sister because snack time is our favorite meal of the day.

We both enjoyed our snacks while we watched television.

Drawings from Majida and Morenikeh:

Meet The Authors

Majida is a five-year-old who loves to read and challenge herself in anything that she does. Majida gained an interest in reading at the age of 2 and started reading full sentences at the age of three. Majida enjoys dressing up, wearing tutus with headbands, and cooking in her kitchen. Majida wants to be a ballerina when she grows up. Her favorite color is pink. Majida enjoys drawing, reading to her little sister, and teaching her new things.

Morenikeh is a vibrant three-year-old who is curious and wants to do everything by herself. Morenikeh is learning through her big sister by repeating every word, sentence, and thing that her sister does. Morenikeh loves to follow her big sister around the house. Morenikeh loves to watch Peppa Pig and Baby Shark. Morenikeh favorite color is green, and that is because when she was learning her colors every color was green. Morenikeh enjoys playing outside, running, kicking a ball, and playing with dirt if we allow her.